# Combing the Snakes
# from His Hair

# Combing the Snakes from His Hair

POEMS BY

## James Thomas Stevens

Michigan State University Press
East Lansing

⊛The paper used in this publication meets the minimum requirements of
ANSI/NISO Z39.48–1992 (R 1997) (Permanence of Paper).

Michigan State University Press
East Lansing, Michigan 48823–5202

Printed and bound in the United States of America.

07 06 05 04 03 02   1 2 3 4 5 6 7 8 9 10

LIBRARY OF CONGRESS CATALOGING-IN-PUBLICATION DATA

Stevens, James Thomas, 1966–
Combing the snakes from his hair: poems / by James Tomas Stevens.
p. cm. — Native American Series (East Lansing, Mich)
ISBN 0-87013-590-2 (pbk..: alk. paper)
1. Iroquois Indians — Poetry. 1. Title. 11. Series.
PS3619.T48 C66 2001    00008705

Cover artwork by David Cusick
Cover design by Heather L. Truelove
Book design by Valerie Brewster, Scribe Typography

Visit Michigan State University Press
on the World Wide Web at:
www.msupress.msu.edu

For M. M.—
One hundred senses blossom
and one hundred emotions contend.

# Contents

## A Half-breed's Guide
## to the Use of Native Plants

5

# Notes on the Music
# I Never Heard

## 67

# Tokinish

## 105

# Acknowledgments

Grateful acknowledgment to the following publications, in which these poems have previously appeared, often in earlier versions: "Sustaining This Massive Shade" in *The Alembic*; "Volley," "The Lure Series," and the first section of "Notes on the Music I Never Heard" in *First Intensity.*

Sincere thanks to the Lockwood Memorial Library of University at Buffalo for the etching from Cusick's *Sketches of Ancient History of the Six Nations.*

"Tokinish" appeared as a chapbook published by Shuffaloff Press in conjunction with First Intensity Press, Staten Island, New York; it also appeared in *Visit Tipi Town: Native Writings After the Detours* (Minneapolis, Minn.: Coffeehouse Press, 1999).

I wish to thank the Mrs. Giles Whiting Foundation and the Kansas Arts Commission. Special thanks to the Stevens family, Trish Reeves, Todd Shryock, Alex Westerfelt, Michael Veit, and Haskell Indian Nations University.

# Introduction

The greatest forces in my life have been language and love. It is language that has allowed me to make the connections I require with all things: the natural, the human, the stories and most importantly, history. Swirling about us all is history—a history that we struggle to make sense of and find relevance to. Often I look to historical texts to read how others have made it through. These writings inspire me, even when they exhibit the darkest side of man. What is my place in all of this? What can I learn?

These poems attempt to center me between nature, love, and history. As a child of mixed-blood heritage, half-Mohawk and half-Welsh, I grew up in an Anglo community but was centered between the Akwesasne Mohawk Reservation (birthplace of my grandmother), the Tuscarora Reservation (home of my grandparents) and the Six Nations Reserve in Ontario (birthplace of my grandfather). Perhaps this drafted the triangular plan I would follow.

The following poems fit this triangular form. Three long poems, beginning with "A Half-breed's Guide to the Use of Native Plants," moving to "Notes on the Music I Never Heard," and ending with "Tokinish," form the three angles. The short verse poems in between are the overlap. They are essentially love poems and they bind all else together. It is only through them that I can begin to create a place for myself to stand.

# A Half-breed's Guide
# to the Use of Native Plants

For centuries the *Haudenosaunee* have looked to plants
for their medicinal properties. The *Kahniakehaka* or
Mohawk sought out the choke cherry and crab apple,
acorn shell and birch bark. The *orenda* or life-force
(for lack of a better translation) came to the aid of
our people. I, too, look to plants for inspiration. Not
the flora of my native northeast, but displaced, I look
to the plants of the Midwest prairie. I look to them
for a key to surviving this new *old world*—a world
that half my blood fought to obtain and the other
half struggled to hold.

*Eryngium yuccifolium*

RATTLESNAKE MASTER

If I clasp my arms in
solitary and unreaching
who will come to  me

                    on this droughted plain?

Like veins in anger thickening,
strong cords running along the margins.

                    I frighten all and attract none
but him who would bite me on the thigh
                  and leave me for dead in the morning.

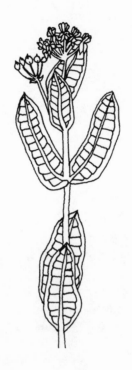

*Asclepias sullivantii*
PRAIRIE MILKWEED

Thick-hearted and sessile
Even his body exhibits a callous core.
Pink at the midrib and
                          alkaline bitter.

You can take much from him
in small doses.
Learn much
                          in spite of him.

But keep the experience as physic
a serum against those who may wrong you.

*Cacalia plantaginea*
INDIAN PLANTAIN

Native in the truest sense,
parallel veins for strength.

Forced to turn a white face
                    to the sun,
to calcify roots in soil
                    yours  and  not  yours.

Indian in that most interior place.

*Aster sericeus*

SILKY ASTER

Proud of slender
                    brown-red limbs.
Some gifts are only visible
when the scales have fallen.

Naked and blossoming
                    in undisturbed lands.

*Cirsium discolor*

PASTURE THISTLE

Bristling outward
his sadism roots him deepest.
Some will hurt whomever they choose.

God-headed and radiant
        but shimmering little to offer.
Don't build your bed of crisis
        or lie on the down of his ire.

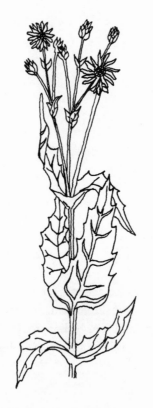

*Silphium perforliatum*
CUP PLANT

With abundant heads for reason
                and open-handed,
growth comes easily
                in fluent fields or dust.
Others will come with long tongues pulling,
cooled from the wellsprings of pathos.

*Coreopsis palmata*
PRAIRIE COREOPSIS

Stiff-necked
and triple-toothed
        at the tips of their tongues,
beautiful ones form colonies
exclusive of others.

Take note
that even in selective groups
it is only those
                        forced to perimeters
that offer up gifts,
        play ing host to beauty.

*Sisyrinchium albidum*
BLUE-EYED GRASS

Slender and wiry
        his unnatural azure draws me
from dense wood to stable prairie.

Inherently enemy
        but the one I love the most.

*Trust me — I set deep roots.*
But always mindful,
his eyes can turn alkaline white.

*Carex meadii*

MEAD'S SEDGE

The fens, the stream, the calcareous swale.
Genetically learned,
arms sway in departure.

Stay near
          the water's edge promise,
the escape, the whisper of better things.

To seek out the liquid
          eyes of your lover,
the mouth ringed with moisture
that shimmers at dawn.

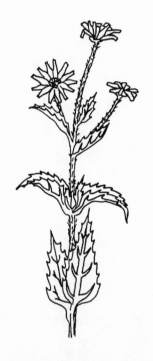

*Heliopsis helianthoides*

FALSE SUNFLOWER

Beautiful from a distance
and prominently toothed,
his radiant head across the prairie.

Your hand against his spine
reveals the coarseness of his skin

and

worse the forked tongue
a fertile forked pistil.

Take note of his tendency to colonize.

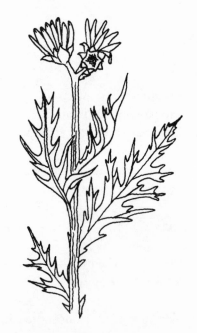

*Silphium laciniatum*
COMPASS PLANT

Some nihilists due to nature
and offspring unable,
are left to direct others
                    pointing out beauty.
And yet so full of desire
the resin runs freely.

Still a few manage, as shining examples
till the pest comes nagging about the neck
and ancient heads droop
                    and die in their infancy.

*Psoralea tenuiflora*

SCURFY PEA

Some survive however they must,
remaining small on the landscape
        to  reduce transpiration.
Changing skins
        to curb reactions,
they  keep shallow roots and break from base.
Dispersing in danger,
        to flee infestation.

*Baptisia leucophaea*

CREAM WILD INDIGO

Others find other means to endure,
hook-like they hang
on the hides of the enemy.
Pollinated by Queens walking across their backs
and  gleaned of precious nectars.
Still they survive
beneath a widely branched crown.
And this,
better than extinction.

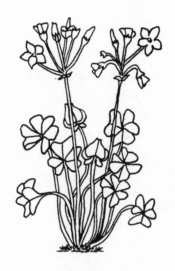

*Oxalis violacea*

VIOLET WOOD SORREL

Lacking a body,
he emerges directly—a  naked heart.
Brilliantly  violet
when others drip golden
but downwardly folding at grey.

He gives  it all  too quickly
then explosively scatters his affections.
Hidden—his sour and acid core.

*Prenanthes aspera*
ROUGH WHITE LETTUCE

Stiff and upright,
from one swollen self,
pubescent and jealous
                    of his own smooth skin.
Beware of the lover
who keeps beauty for himself,
weaving his fingers
                    to enclose his light within.

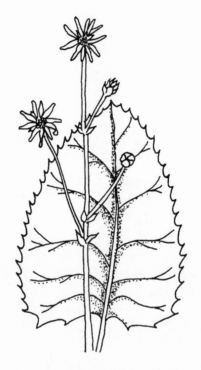

*Silphium terebinthinaceum*

PRAIRIE DOCK

Coarse skinned and heady
       with  the scent of turpentine
and lacking the lustre
that glimmers across the field,
he stands heavily rooted
       and devoted to the soil.

When others lose their beauty
and fall to the seasons,
       he will stand alone
to rebuild from the ashy waste.

*Lithospermum canescens*
PRAIRIE PUCCOON

Wise but guarded
                and wisdom glittering,
some keep their gifts for the few
with interest enough to pry them.

And when they go
you search their empty rooms
to find seeds of knowledge
                like pieces of polished bone.

*Gentiana andrewsii*

BOTTLE GENTIAN

Seductively  smooth and parallel-veined
his skin is like a map
                without a key.
Downwardly bending and blue.
Be sure of your strength
before you wrest the beauty from him.

Few can hold the door open
and fewer escape.

*Castilleja coccinea*

INDIAN PAINT BRUSH

With varied characteristics
from a single strong line,
the colors of  a  people
are painted across the landscape.

Flourishing twice in their time
—the second bloom about to open.
Let artists and writers
prepare the canvas.

And leaving the prairie with empty hands, what I take in gifts is threefold. Therein lies the knowledge of the body, heart and mind. The secrets of random beauty, told in the colors of prairie tapestry.

I have learned a way of contentment with my body. My hand, which had sprouted five fingers at birth, lost three to the blade but growth moved elsewhere, the other became stronger. Taught by the untapped side of my mind, the instinct to survive drought and injury forced new limbs — branches of understanding. The last I saw my father before his death, closed-eyed, he held my broken hand in his own. He rubbed the bend of my finger and recognized the lines. Now surprised and thankful for this cold blessing.

Here the heart, where I must accept the random blessing. Consider the garden I had planned so carefully, some came up too early and others not at all. The years are unpredictable and strange winds bring strange seeds. Some rough and blue, like the chicory that outshines the cultured hybrid. Some sharp and resentful as prairie nettle. Then in February, a new seed comes and you say we feel like rain after years of dry discomfort. And didn't the augur see you, falling from the wings of a bird.

The mind is the hardest crop to tend. The simple design of the Cup Plant reminds me that reserves of cool water draw others to drink. But dry and jealous, I am often empty—with nothing but dust to offer. Maybe accepting what comes is the answer to growth, the acceptance of deaths, small and large. The acceptance of love is often hardest to learn, sympathetic with the wax leaf repelling the rain. But let me accept this random beauty, then unquestioningly give it away.

# That I Knew You Would Return

So long as there's a hill-ridge somewhere the dreamer
Can place his land of marvels
W.H. AUDEN

Why they live here, I know and I don't
but these Kansas plains make me weep and regret
that you're away and if you were here
the land wouldn't have hidden its every color
or given up blue, even as the father of green
to embroider the ravines with tufts of gray.

A man minus another is not a disadvantage,
too wrestling here
with wants but knowing the nature of things
too well to be caught in the wanting.

And not one silo yellowed when the sun lifted
its childish head over the horizon.
As it is, though, the avoidance
of an image of you I can and can't remember,
naked in the candlelight.
I should hate us all till the image returns.

# The Act of God

*for Michael*


And when I woke in the night scratching at ghost skins
I fell asleep recounting how to tie knots
as if lack were temporary and regeneration near.
Wishing now, I'd paid them more attention
in their four guiltless years, taken the time
to memorize the comfort of company
inside a deerskin mitten.

Recalling nothing but red, a thumb dangling in may,
the old mower grinds to a decisive halt.
Oh perfect little starfish at the end of my arm, torn
and sewn badly, startling swollen white.
What is left to mourn? Three tiny fingers thrown
against a chain link fence? A hand's own memory
of having been more?

How it all led to the moment when I became bad.
Irrelevant details, yet all running in the same direction.
I was a child, they should have known better but
they laid hands on me and prayed in tongues that
smelled of hot lamps and praise projected on a wall.
Some children are named *bad* for taking
what's not theirs, but I am bad for not taking what was offered.
They said I was denying god's gift of regrowth
but I was accepting the absence of god.

And thirty years later I still wake searching
not for fingers more like acquaintance, but
for you who laid by me so many times longer,
who was there when I ran from that botched healing
down the river road along the greasy niagara.

And in the back room of the night marina
smelling of gasoline and smoke,
you wrapped me in rabbit skins, holding my face
to your pale neck.

# Where I Went This Evening

These moods come
likening themselves to the moment
you were first aware
of a new lover's breath
whistling through the dark pitcher of your throat.

Aware of a certain clarity
and sensing delicate blue
only morning glories should know.

                    Overcome and sentient.
                    You climb, a viney braid
                    to entwine his fine legs and fix
                    long fingers at the small of the back.

This is the awkward dance of a garden.

Of rarest moods
that bend the exhausted trellis of ease.

# Lure

The rain, its tiny pressure
against us
and the mid-west sky
                scratching its stomach
above.

You could never know
what it is            I feel looking
while you sleep
like a man
                who scarce propels his boat
against the stream

and I can not keep from touching
                the impossible white
then the startling carpet
                of gold beneath your arm.

To know you are here
is a way through
                        the dropping wind
that moves then tires
                at this seductive task.

# Left

Primordial silt beneath the red-buds,
growing easy to remember,
A yellow tongue cracked         from the center of the bloom.
It was the last time I saw you.
You felt the bent of my finger
and I knew you knew a shore

                      other than that

the trestle reached for.


Nothing salt-licked or seaweed
but the din of rails

              or a spoon clamoring

between your teeth.


Along this river, beneath these clouds,
I hate most that you don't know        where I am.
Rain while dogs leap
by an aching iron bridge.

# Kaw

A grain elevator explodes into silence

lying in — beside you
The impossible whiteness
      beneath your arm.
Stumbled in
      the superabundant harvest.
Late between clavicles
      the tillage meets the shore.

I am touched by the insensitivity
      you show toward my pressing,
crushed by your locks
      tumbling loudly in my sleep.

# Burrow

Here, the seething of estuaries
What is this place?
Longing to touch
in this unsexed space,
                    the shoulder
I saw where I stood from behind.
Two small marks
                    at the base of your neck,
I am sure that even you
don't know exist.
How they remind me of the clay
                    along cradleland rivers.
Vague and smooth
I have never seen legs like yours,
recalling paths traced through silt.
Rise like the river
                    after rain.

# Windmark

Winding your way
like perverted acts in pastures.

Even the sound of your current
is an obstacle.
Back to back at a bar
        heat flows from your skin
lambent white,
        the new sycamore.
Gorges of blossoms
from your whiskered jaw.

How can I feed you
and learn the tendance

        that your kind of tree requires.

# Unbeknownst

If only I knew what it is you really want,
not what you spend hours
telling me that you want but
the thing that makes you pass out in front of the fire
eidered down in wood chips and
your hand shakes even in a state of sleep
and you don't know what to do for lack of moving
from place to place.
And what if
I placed my hand in your hair
and you saw a river for the first time
bearing hollow ships.

# Sustaining This Massive Shade

Of all that is left to occur
when nothing moves
but beneath my skull
                    a dog stretches tremulous forelegs.
Cicadas drone in every tendon
while the wind offers nothing
                    to keep insects from the skin.
And still he returns
like the new leaf unfurling.

                              In sum, what nightfall has in store.

*I keep four calendars* he said.

Beneath one moon

                              I am jealous.

Of all that touches him,
the rain that doesn't fall
        and the woman that lies next to him.
In this age of hands,
where are mine.
I am intact and I don't care.

My hands in the garden.
Corn bleached
            and malformed by drought
beneath the sick of blue.

## 2

*I have the white-blue eyes of my ancestors* he said,
*their narrow skull and their clumsiness in fighting.*

Fighting to keep my hand from his belly
                      where sleeps a double sex.
Struggling not to touch
                      the small bones held in by sandals,
I take note of his every step.

Given confidence
and confiding in the agave.
            The cactus mourns the memory of feeling
and mysterious delicacies seduce me.

That this night would give up

                                   one breath

to stir the downy hairs on his golden legs.
The skin that aches
            for want of feather.

## 3

How I move between rooms,
                  the cattle of longing
and think only of that curve
                  at the base of his skull.

The cowlick clipped
            to a choirboy's mean halo.

*I am happy* he said.

                                   I am jealous.

Of the planets
that seduce him with greater success
and that moon that lights his pale arm
when he rises in the night.


*Walk through the night, gently moving that thigh, that second thigh,*
*And that left leg.*

# For Lack of Your Delicate Hip

Sullen and anxious, I rose last night while others kept right on sleeping,
braving winds against the nightmare, walking first to the dark counter for a
      glass of wine
and on to the garden to consider that feverless spot beside me
where last night you lay for the first time in my arms.

Lighting a fire in the chimney pot, I pulled blackened stems from last year's
yield of sunflowers and considered the day. How walking down the street,
      the mechanical count of parking meters clamored in my ears, weighing
      the time
till we could lie again, your long foot pressed against my leg.

And while those life gone stalks turned to ember, I watched the fine hair roots
that burned most quickly, the tiny miracles I had resigned myself to
      for nourishment.
Cinders that night fashioned into words you whispered
when I last held you. Cinders that caught in the leaves of our thinking,
lighting the garden  and allowing notice of the thoughtfulness of tulips
to raise their heads in February.

# Volley

Aware that sudden fires,
like clouds come often at night,
I move to undo your thigh
and absent years dwindle
                    like cinders above the water.
But small birds
slip from branches at the salvo,
                    waiting for the sky to fall.

# Nightwatch

There were those who impudently asserted that this decree
had its origin not in judicious inquiry, but in passion none
too well informed.

GALILEO

Yesterday
we resolved to meet today,
                              revolving
around the impossibility of hypothesis.


You've made me a globe like a planet.
Unalterable and silent
                              beneath your system,
held in the greatest slowness.
Afraid, even to place my hand against yours.


The unattainable in threefold dimension.


Not merely the line that I could trace, a cold finger moving across your
shoulders after a rainstorm, nor a bare surface, the plane of your
chest, cold and taut. But a body having length, breadth, and depth.
Outlined in front of the window, your wholeness is concluded. I
have nowhere else to go.


Transition is made according to defect.


Not to admit that you have none,
a tooth turned too slightly, or the gentle arch of your legs.
Through imperfection, the perfect transition.


You attribute too much to numbers    and I too little.


But I've taken count
of the fine hairs that divide your belly,

and I'm scared to reveal
the most hidden properties of these numbers.

I want to remain common where facts are concerned,
because my comprehension lies in your numbers,
the length of your arm and the circumference of your eye.
The celestial and elemental,
met in its revolution.

# Mismaloya

When it happened the first night
                    staring over Banderas Bay
it was like discovering myself awake
while everyone else was sleeping.


And even the moon slept pressed
                  behind a cloud's cool thigh,
creating a screen of perfect black
on which to play and replay
your laughing eyes and teeth
           behind lips drawn back
                    in uncensored delight.


And Mexican men and women
rose from night-dampened sheets
                  tethering their dogs
that yelped and howled at an image of you
rising above the bay.

# Augury

Of the random turning of birds in flight
marking auspicious, the moment we touched beneath the table
that these feelings would rise unaccountable
to others who took no note of the night,
or the unsleeping gravity that drew me to your side.
Within two days—within two arms, this destination attainable.
The miracle, that entwined we are still able
to maneuver through this torrential light.

To rise each morning and watch the sun
as it spreads from pale foot to golden brow,
is to envy its ability to touch you completely.
Jealous of the birds that saw you come
from the no where to the now here.
The way they must have laughed at me.

# Notes on the Music
# I Never Heard

Music heard so deeply
that it is not heard at all, but you are the music
while the music lasts.

T.S. ELIOT, *The Dry Salvages*

# Notes on the Music I Never Heard

The note binds us,
                     at distant corners
with the melancholy of brilliant tandem
                            arrangement,
twinned with the natural
                           resonance of
your ear.

Now, its geographical training.


Vibrations gleaned,
            and later transcribed,

the way I benefit from your reading
each night beneath fingertips
                          educated of ivories,
transformed by touch.


Observed,
             a twitching eyelid
revolving cyclical to a new note.

To translate emotion after the concerto, is to re-assess
the pulse of your neck, transformed by pitch that is still
just pulsating air, the stirring of molecules, answered
by your skin.


The triple canals of your ear
                    allow you balance
irrigation by the wet-note,
                    I enter in.


To watch your face, at the resolve of *The Tempest*
                    is to comprehend emotion,
through ocular melody.


Thin grimace of pleasure along the trill.

II.

I could comprehend perhaps,
the music through terminology,

you might explain each step of a tumbling strain
or the demand for modulation
if in doing so it didn't destroy pure thought.


Who would split firewood with a razor?

                    —Heimholtz, *Sensation of Tone*


but the man who discounts music,
*that has no foundation in science or system,*
who said of *Barbarians,*
*their best music is said to be hideous and astonishing.*

                    —Sir John Hawkins,
           *General History of the Science and Practice of Music*

As if complexity of culture and composition
were equivocal.


The size of a tribe's characteristic step
was attributed to this factor:

             *The narrower the step, the narrower the mind.*

71

III.

A red hand resting across white thighs,

                              murmuring tensions

of sinew and skin,
said violin of human thought.


Strained to reach a crescendo,

                              alternation of touch

where it demands after all,
a certain balance of two notes,

                              exact in weight and gravity,

your body against mine.


We, the musically primitive,
when placed side by side.

The song from your skin,

                              logogenic, spontaneous

composed of scent,
surrounded by chanting.


Rhythm when now you are far from here.

Vienna 6th October, 1777

I feel sad at times because I cannot hear you playing the clavier and
violin, and each time I come home a faint melancholy falls upon me,
for as I draw near to our house I always half expect to hear the strains of
your fiddle.

— Leopold Mozart to Wolfgang


To become the hall or home
                    that houses the echo,
a grand piano behind mud walls.
Your city was an opera
                    where mine was a drum.

But comparison denotes a method only,
and not a branch of learning.

Education can begin at the closing of an eye.

IV.

A red hand resting against your chest
                                senses rhythm inherent,
broadcast through bone.

I understand your rhythm
because it is born of the body,
                                corporeal and calm.

Narrative, its beat
                    is the conscious art of illustration.

Though primitive,
it needs no horn to signal the hunt
                    or a frenzied cadenza signifying success.


The story is there to pass unheard
by post-primitive scholars and science alike.

Without instrument
        what can be written?

But isn't the instrument an extension of the body, a supplement to the hand that slaps the thigh in its quest to find rhythm, and in rhythm alleviation? Transfusion from the moving limb, the impulse to equalize, extends outwards through percussion, the inroad to calm.

Rhythm in its beginnings is extramusical.
                                 —Curt Sachs, *The Wellsprings of Music*

v.

But this and your body shape two separate arts,
working together, an inborn symphony.

Subtle conditionings of musical enculturation
have taught me to hear you
                                        as advanced in your song.


Whisper of bird notes,
                        the fall of the oar
and I will move the symphony
                                to mean color
                                        and its corresponding pitch.



You say music as an art
                        requires time,
a temporal space in which
                        to hear the succession of notes,

yet I can sense the entirety of your body at once
                                or enjoy the individual movement of its parts.

You are polyphony and monotone,
                        the primary and its shade.

Where colors cannot occupy the same space
                              without change,
when occupying space next to one another,
they remain separate,
                    affected, but still individual.


Notes can occupy simultaneous space,
                        recognizable to a point.
You said it takes time to hear the music through,
that immediacy is lost
                    in the *we*
                              and the music.



   ... and the whole, though it be long, stands almost complete and
finished in my mind, so that I can survey it, like a fine picture or a
beautiful statue, at a glance. Nor do I hear in my imagination the
parts successively, but I hear them, as it were, all at once ( *gleich
alles zusammen*).

—Wolfgang Amadeus Mozart

## VI

All at once
    I move to shadow
        for a better view of music,

to allow scope
through darkness, a reversal of laws.


You have closed your eyes
to the cacophony of sight,
removing the detail to catch a glimpse of form.



When here the opposite is true.
A black room above the river,
magnifies
each detail of your body.

Each downy hair
        springing upward after touch,
like the field that records the shape of the fawn,

blade by blade, obstinate in its resurrection.


I found in the steady meter of your breathing
        a timepiece far away . . .


Metronomic,
    there is no harmony
just rhythm deemed *primitive,*
        an immaculate fiction

that resists transcribing.

> Not because music is too vague, but rather too precise to translate
> into words.
>
> —Felix Mendelssohn


In your mind, the scores
        that should for these reasons
be too numerous for remembrance,
are there to be called up
        with your own intentions.


Here I call a garden
        like a transcript in the yard
ordered in its looseness,
        open to interpretation.

You know you have sown
                    a row of blue dahlias
ending in a cadenza
            of cosmos yellowed orange.

But each spring plays it differently
for a snow fallen late.

The purpled othello
                    might bloom first,
having read design in a different way.

Variations on a theme
                    or order at rest.

Played against the garden wall,
a string of blue morning glories,
different by moonlight
                    or the opening of the sun.

Ordered by genetics
            but open to accident,
a hand that had five fingers
                    has lost three to the blade,
but you taught me which notes to sacrifice
and still retain the whole.


Who fixed the *Moonlight Sonata* but not the inconstant moon?

## VII

Where you are my reference to the music
and I cannot hear you play,
irreference is workable and a useful tool,

      if held within its limitations.

And I cannot know what I have missed
away from the garden,

      behind walls. They are yours.


                       29th June 1778
   . . . and you can easily imagine that it is a species of martyrdom
to me to know that he has composed much during all this time,
while I, unhappily, can hear nothing of that which was once my
chiefest delight.
                         −Leopold Mozart to Wolfgang

A species of martyrdom
          to misunderstand
what it is you feel sleeping,
          my hand against your mouth.


It is rhythm amplified
against the thick skin of scars,
a drum stretched tighter across the years.


The river, below the bedroom
          sounds the leitmotif of union,
there as a frame
to hold these notes together.

Your arms in my arms
                are the encumbered coastline,


charted by the listener
                across the continents of lullaby.



Functioning as we do in two different localities,
sleeping between our differences
                and waking to that burden.

That sound itself is seductive,
whether violin or voice,

you could raise me to frenzy
                    (or lull me to sleep),
the peaceful spreading
                    of the glory in your faith.




Circling stars,
lulled across borders
on the seduction of sound itself.

The promise of harmony
playing prelude to the conquest.

## VIII.

History allies itself,
        to you and I,
not in conquest,
        but obsession — its musical means.

Monogamy and polyphony,
a city rose and fell.


            Myself, or Tenochtitlan



A painted people across the shores
where colours could not occupy
        the same space without change.

Can a people remain separate,
        affected, yet still individual?
Can I tell you of choirs
        greater than your own,
        previous to yours,
not here but there.

There, in a desert
with stones for a skyline.
        The agave before the opera house,
witnessed voice
        converted by passion.

And I didn't sound myself
after you'd carried me to your room.

Polyphonous the breathing,
while Mozart played on.
How continents come together
where histories overlap.

Monotonous rhythms
                like sticks against stone
that were played years before
to appease a god or gods,
                not to blind with musical virtuosity,
your culture against mine.


This preoccupation,
                this return, to understand
the music, the conquest.
                                My body against yours.

IX.

Each skin
inscribed by the other's experience.

What we say to one another,
making us part to the other's history.

A forceful singing to sleep,
rocked into nightmare
                    by a new community of faith.

Passionate and convicted
                    but merciless they move on,
without ears to hear
                    another's strains
unless they match their own.


Where,
                    Fervor, united with keen intelligence, erects a new
                    dogma . . . and it strives to make it serve its own end.
                                    —Schnabel, *Reflections on Music*


As long as the end
leaves favour on their side,

buried beneath
and because of inconsistencies,

a people like a late bulb
that never blooms, come any spring.

x.

Again the garden
            we planted together.
Variegated ivy, the climbing schematic,
punctuated with yucca spires
            or a prickly pear's yellow rose.


Shoulders grow dark
            seeding sunflowers by the wall
and from the cool recess,
            a requiem sounds.



But what can be composed
            of one orange poppy?
Island in a field
            of air-blue blossoms?

A rhythm to match its incremental opening,
or the symphony,
            blaring it into bloom?

Overstatement to the quiet violence
            of a bud splitting open.

A colour comes into existence

all at once
            the people learn your song.

Captured by the beauty
                    of a night-blooming cereus,
traveling,
          from a distance of seven and eight leagues.


While others come
almost equal distance
                    by water to hear the singing.


Where voices reached proportions
your people hadn't known.

Traveling toward music
          we walked the lower river,
traversing time in winter
without complaint
          and the humming fields in summer,
the time to think.


                              Postscript Milan 24 August 1771
     The heat on our journey was very great, and the dust smothered us
     so audaciously that we should doubtless have been choked and
     suffocated if we had not taken care . . .
                              —Wolfgang Amadeus Mozart

. . . to make the move less painful
to terracotta streets.

Care
    to hear the vihuelas strum,
the murmur of invention . . .        The  Flute--------The Cocoloctli.


Sentiment that joined instrument
to the fragile web of birth,
                            the hollow reed reverberating
against a spider's timpanous sack.
Vibrato
        pulled from the web wellspun,
drawn into the din of symphony.


Violin - - - - - - - - - - - - - - -Vihuelas
Viola - - - - - - - -and - - - - - -Tlapitzali
Cello - - - - - - - - - - - - - -Quitzquitzli
Flute - - - - - - -and - - - - -Cocoloctli
Oboe - - - - - - - - - - - - - -Cacalachtli
Clarinet - - - - - -and - - - - - -Coyolli
Snare Drum - - - - - - - - - - - - -Ayotl
Kettle  - - - - - -and - - - - -Huehuetl


Experience has shown how greatly edified the Indians are by
polyphony, and how fond they are of music in general. More than
by preaching, the Indians are converted by music. They come from
great distances to hear it, and they work hard to learn it and to
become proficient in it.
                        —Juan de Zumarraga, 1st Bishop of Mexico

Proficient at loss
    and fearing retrogression.


The oval note of the water drum
and rasp of your forearm
      against my face.
Lost, the branches of aria
      composed by storm,
the song of your torso
      lifting in pleasure.


    The joy of music is the soul's delight in being invited to recognize
    itself in the body.
                      —Claude Levi-Strauss, *The Naked Man*


These, the transcripts
    in the archives of synapse.

XII.

Sleeping cruciform
      on the bed,
I cannot escape your symbol.


But the stringed cross,
lyre or lyric—
      the golden wires beneath your arm
resonate colours of flower and song.


Sad Quetzacoatl sways,
a feathered serpent beneath you belly.


Withered—the cacao trees
      turned to mesquite.


The  inlaid masks earthed
where no pale hands can unearth them.

Mounds in the cradlelands
    clinging tight to the coast.


Northward, the builders
carrying flutes along the way.

Kneeling on the isthmus
at the foot of the great island

        Your golden feet from beneath the sheets,
        I look to for perfection, not for piety.



        Rome, 14th April, 1770
    Now I have been drawing Saint Peter with his keys, Saint Paul
with his sword, together with Saint Luke, etc.; and I have had
the honour of kissing Saint Peter's toes in Saint Peter's . . .
        —Wolfgang Mozart



But the rose window of verdure
shimmering between spires of pine
        the only cathedral.

Rubbing legs together,
creating gardens of  song


      where from the blossoms of harmony,

        flaming birds take flight in sorrow.

# A Tale of the Foundation of the Great Island

*with apologies to David Cusick*

*Among the ancients there were two worlds in existence. The lower world was in a great darkness; but the upper world was inhabited by mankind; and there was a woman conceived and would have the twin born.*

I want to take your hand off your hip, because standing there you look
  like art.
But this is how I see you, beside the river, at least metaphorically, where
  they can't see us.
Wanting to kiss your perfect ear, standing out from your head like the
  marbled Tecumseh.
Afraid they'd see our world, where beauty means something, a sculpted
  vein inside your arm.

*She was induced by some of her relations to lay herself on a mattrass which was prepared; but while she was asleep the very place sunk down towards the dark world.*

But I'm stuck in a traffic of birds and branches, afraid you won't come over
And the bed looks so nice today, because of the spring sun. You arrive
and I ask if you won't lie down. Your body like a mattress on a mattress,
gives with my weight where you expect me to fall.

*Descending to the lower world; all the species of the creatures were immediately collected into where it was expected she would fall.*

I never considered you'd scream from the window, but the eyes of
laundering neighbors gather in judgement. And I'm wondering why you
didn't choose the pillow. A mouth full of down, the arrival silenced. But
there you are looking like art again. Your well curved arches lifting to the
light, about to betray this world of kind men.

*Who would be capable to secure the woman from the great water, but none was able to comply except a large turtle came forward and made proposal to them to endure her lasting weight, which was accepted.*

I don't want the fluorescent hum, but candles. And you're beautiful while
    the clawfoot fills.
Step in. Lie down. Legs tangled in the design that this tub requires. I
want to rest my head on your floating belly, and forget the neighbor
circling paradise on a riding mower.

*While holding her, the turtle increased every moment and became a considerable island of earth, and apparently covered with small bushes.*

Resting and satisfied, it's hard to believe that out there could be any
vacation spot I'd rather visit. Forget Ile de la Cité or even Manhattan,
that grows with every lifting brick. I'm satisfied here, gazing off at your
neck in the distance. The hedge row and hedge apple dividing the view.

*One of the infants in her womb was moved by an evil opinion and he was determined to pass out under the side of the parent's arm, and the other infant in vain endeavored to prevent his design.*

I want to rest beneath your arm while the tub fills with darkness, my
cheek against a mossy carpet. But I'm moved by twinned desires: for you
to lie here simply breathing or walk naked under the kitchen lamp. And
the thought of you wet and alone on the linoleum is evolution in design.
I want to move and let you rise, but stayed in the porcelain oval of your
arms, I struggle with my decision.

*The infants entered the dark world by compulsion, and they had the power of sustenance without a nurse, and remained in the dark regions.*

Outside the streetlights flicker to life, mapping our island through the venetian blinds. And I'm hungry and you're hungry, so we're forced to surface. The air is so cold and the kitchen lamp so bright, but I love how you look walking naked with one hand raised to cover your eyes. Adam trying to flee the garden, where guilty, I follow behind.

# Three Translations from the Mohawk

*Teiohonwa:ka ne'ni akhonwe:ia. Kon'tatieshon iohnekotatie. Wakkawehatie, wakkawehatie.*

The canoe is very fast. It is mine. All day I hit the water. I paddle along. I paddle along.

I am the hull—rapid against your stream.
Birch beneath the ribs
        circumnavigating your body.

Endless propeller of my arm
        as it circles to find the flow.

I move this way against you.
I move this way.

# MOSQUITO SONG

*Okariata:ne tahotharatie. Tahsakohroria:ne ne tsi niho:ten. Ne se aonha:a*
*thorihwaka:ion. Ne se aonha:a thoriwaka:ion.*

The mosquito is bringing a message. He comes to tell us how poor he is.
In truth, he is repetative and brings the same old message.


A voice returns
                    to tell these things.
Of unencumbered arms.

Returns to remind me
                    in truth          —          I am alone.

Sleeping through the din
                    of  solitude's stinging messenger.

## CORNBREAD SONG

*Kana'tahrokhon:we teiothwe'non:ni. Ne se ni:'i kwa wake:kahs.*
*Kana'tahrokhon:we teiothwe'non:ni. Onkwehon:we ronon:ni.*

This cornbread is round. I like it. This cornbread is round. The Indian
people form it.


Circular we move
to create
        the seminal form.

Pleasured but saddened
        creating a circle only.

The principle,
for people
        to give it form.

Lamenting,
        we simply lay.

# The Ritual of Condolence

## I. TEARS OR ONE'S EYES

Uninvited this knowledge, but privilege at once.
The way we take things in unintentionally, without the wanting.
The countless times I took you in, like an image
of light on the barn from the windows of your childhood home.
Knowing the pain of farmstead and father. Uninvited history.
Now you're gone and this dumb knowledge might have
finished my faculties, if I hadn't rallied to see it
as something like damage, lying black at the edge of the ashpit.

## II. EARS OR HEARING

At times I lived like a man obstructed, hearing nothing
of what was taking place on earth, but focused on the flush
of blood to manyed parts. But at least I know
when I lost faith in myself. Desert November, a lover left
not saying goodbye, though I knew it was
because the russian olive dropped all its leaves at once.
I threw the dog from my bed and he limped for days.
Fearing fracture, never again to trust myself,
sentenced to hear the cry of all things broken.

## III. THROAT

Of all that rises from that deep pitcher,
throat of the flesh body sorely obstructed. When he died
I went to the river and called him, like a man from the field at suppertime.
And the air was filled — with the prevalence of absence.
And now you leave and when I cry it sounds like pure adolescence,
a simple choking and throttling, embarrassing and shaming.
Red-faced and angered, stroking sore Adam's apple.
This knot I feel is the sum of my words, collected in this place.

## IV. WITHIN HIS BREAST

The disordered and wrenched, within bed and breast.
Emotions thrown off in a night of fevered dreaming
lay tangled on the hardwood among strands of your hair
but today began the work of reorganization
and I broke every cup you ever raised to your mouth.
I replaced the heart between the lungs,
straightened the spleen, the liver in order.
But the heart looked like a queer new building
standing in place of one once familiar
which even now, I cannot recall.


## V. THE BLOODY HUSK-MAT BED

As a boy I created wounded men in fields behind the house,
dragging them to safety beneath sumac mounds.
I made mud to set broken limbs and held bleeding hands.
And when I grew older, I found a mourning dove
fallen from its nest too early. Careful not to move it,
I forced worm's meat inside its beak.
In the night I heard danger and walked barefoot to the yard,
searching sightless till I felt my own sick weight
displace that feathered vault of heaven.
And I fell to the grass—a doctor undone
sitting cross-legged in wretchedness.


## VI. THE DARKNESS OF GRIEF

Consumed by thick darkness itself, the night plane
seen from field or highway is absolute grief.
A miniature blinking, the only sign
of two hundred lives hurtling through coldest night.
And I always weep for the libraries that could be lost,
the lives perilously seated within my own head
transported through the night
on a cold pillow in a cold room where

momentary clouds flash outside windows wet with rain
reminiscent of the qualities of light on this earth.


## VII. THE LOSS OF THE SKY

At first I expected you every night after
and left the door unlocked. Your night ride across the east
to enter while I slept. Waking to your unexpected body,
a hunger historically ours, though
unable to fix the coming day's discord.
And the sky packed all its things and left
like a lover who leaves because he told you he would
and not because he wants to.
Now you and the sky are lost to my view,
unprivileged to know what takes place in either.


## VIII. HIS SUN IS LOST

Outside the screendoor, a car stares blindly.
Behind it, a house, bent pole for a clothesline,
and behind that, another house, and dogs, always dogs.
So easy to misplace the movement of the sun.
This morning I found it in the woods, aware of its drawing
nearer and nearer to me, and I loved you again
in every branch against my arm, realizing
the city creates an artificial loathing,
and you become another thing to get done.
But today I burned the houses where they stood,
and attached the sun again in its place.


## IX. THE HEAP OF CLAY ON THE GRAVE

Two different things always take place
during the nights and during the days.
One is the steaming discomfort of vision,
the other the drizzle of the one denied,
forcing the flowers of insecurity,

where the fat bee feeds at night.
I saw you with a child by one that wasn't me,
and choked on your betrayal, conscious
that it was I who buried all promise,
that the sun and rain should never reach it.
Each morning, I lay on the mound above
pulling up several kinds of grasses.


## X. TWENTY IS THE PENALTY FOR MURDER

The things done, one to the other
for the sake of nightly collision, violent
little death on the battlefield of your thigh,
a white face stained against molding leaves
and pity for your lost homeland, which is you
and the ground—you held before we met.
Giving up, breaking treaties with ourselves
composed at birth, we wake and turn
to seek the other's hands
and bind our bones by twenty strings.


## XI. THE COUNCIL FIRE

Eager for nothing but anticipation,
disappointment lies hard by your lodges at night.
Bodies like scattered firebrands
around the embers of who you meant to be.
You meant to be an artist
and cut off your nimble hands,
you meant to wear braids and
lost your hair at a tender age.
You meant to draw promise to a flame in the clearing
but set it scattering in the brambled stand.

## XII. THE WOMAN AND WARRIOR

I noted the hair at his nape, turning to oily down
the way the sick transform before diving or taking flight.
Preparing a place, he'd smooth the pillow
three times before resting his head;
once for the father, once for the son,
and once for the holy ghost.
He only died once and who can know
what it was she felt waking
to a silence only the planets should know,
entrusting his breath to the becoming.

## XIII. ANYTHING CAN HAPPEN ON EARTH, EVEN INSANITY

Sleepless for the barking of birds,
the dog lays twittering at the foot of the bed.
A slow splash caused by the falling away of the mind,
the thickening slip of clay from a lakeslope.
Strangely excited by this unexpected chance
to form and reform fingers from this red earth.
That when these hands are complete again
the clouds might cease to squirm.

## XIV. THE TORCH OF NOTIFICATION

One poor short day has come repeatedly,
forming a black string of partings.
But each year meeting on the shores of ontario
we place two rods together and fix
a torch between the two, equally owned.
And the way between us remains clean swept,
no trace of lying down on the path.

## XV. THE APPEAL FOR THE CANDIDATE

The place beside me has been caused to be vacant
once more by your insistent memory.
So I raise you up and name you
as the molder of my senses,
appealing to our history
which belongs to northern rivers.
That you would meet me on the slope
with the black strand we've shared
to accept this thinning pouch from my breast
and lie eternal at forest's edge.

# Tokinish

**Tokinish** (tó kin'ish) v. command meaning:
"Wake him."                                    [Narragansett]

Much comfort is not in much sleepe, when the most
fearefull and most irrevocable Malediction is pre-
sented by thee, in a perpetuall sleepe. I will make
their feasts, and I will make them drunke, and they
shall sleepe a perpetuall sleepe, and not wake.

JOHN DONNE, *Devotions upon Emergent
Occasions* FROM *Expostulation XV*

# Tokinish

But yet the body is his book.
DONNE

| | |
|---|---|
| *Awaunkeesitteoúwincohòk?* | Who made you? |
| *Wússuckwheke.* | The book. |

NARRAGANSETT TRANSLATION


To walk the periphery of islands, as if knowing the border of body.
To mould the well-muscled
                curve of your back
modeled of river weeds hanging red on the scarp.
Water run down river rock,
the combe beneath your arm.
          Skin shining stone
               as the sun settles into its own dumb orthodoxy.
Hemlock shoreline,
of trunks forced into silt's precision.

The vegetable earth on a mineral spine.

How to write island, the weighty peninsula of extremities.
The red of lichen on
a head of stone.

Weight is the catastrophe of what we don't know,
                  the unsleeping gravity drawing boat to shore.

*Acâwmuck notéshem.*      I came over the water.

*Mesh nomishoonhómminn.*      I came by boat.

ROGER WILLIAMS
*A Key into the Language of America*

Island.
Look to a map to prove the concept mute.
All waters have a source and this connection renders earth

                                        island.

Is the naked-eye observance of a border

                          in every direction, the thing we call true?
Lack of continuity, the outline of matter.

The island of a leaf in a yellow field of corn,
the island of a bowl, or objects on a table,
the island of a word.
I call your sleeping body island
because I know its white border.

Roger Williams set foot in what would become Providence, Rhode Island in 1636. Because he saw water on all sides he wrongly assumed the land to be island. Although the Native he saw standing before him was certainly isolated in isolated surroundings, he did not call him island.

| *Tocketussawêitch?* | What is your name? |
| *Nníshishem.* | I am alone. |

To say it requires a boat or bridge
to reach a true island
           is to simplify the question too much.
A bridge or boat are simple movement.
When the boat is not moving across, it ceases to be boat
           and a bridge is forever gerund.

*Spanning* implies movement, as when the bridge no longer spans the gap,
it ceases to be that bridge.


My hand as it reaches to touch your belly,
reaching to island or inland, the shallow dome
              and the mossy path
        ( leading
            to secret
               parts.)

What remains secret in the two-fold nakedness
of the explorer,
      the naked find.

| *Paúskesu.* | Naked. |
| *Pauskesítchick.* | Naked men. |
| *Nippóskiss.* | I am naked. |

*They have a two-fold nakednesse:*

*First ordinary and constant, when although they have a Beasts skin, or an English mantle on, yet that covers ordinarily but their hinder parts and all the foreparts from top to toe, (except their secret parts, covered with a little Apron, after the patterne of their and our first Parents) I say all else open and naked.*

*Their second nakednesse is when their men often abroad, and both men and women within doores, leave off their beasts skins, or English cloth, and so (excepting their little Apron) are wholly naked; . . .*

— R.W.

The earth with its skin of beasts,
a forested skin of leaf and bark,
                        the live beast itself becoming skin.

The naked field opening fertile,
                        and fertile forest woodland.

The jagged tops of trees mending
sky to earth,
the interlocking
                that for lack of, separates man from sky
                                        man from man.
Smooth skins that will not bind.

Clay to clay,
the coils of a vessel,
                require the scoring of a jagged stick.

A twisting trail to secret parts,
unclear, most fertile, wild and overgrown. A river flows upward into sky.

| | |
|---|---|
| *Sepûo?* | Is there a river? |
| *Toyusquanûo?* | Is there a bridge? |

Is there a bridge to that part of you, besides the one I call my own? If in definition, the bridge connects two isolated points, then we must decide when I reach to you, which body is isolated? Or is isolation a mutual thing. If in its isolation, there is no recognition of its being "alone," no desire to become part to another, who rightfully calls it "island"?

*The Indians of Martin's vineyard, at my late being amongst them, report generally, and confidently of some Ilands, which lie off from them to Sea, from whence every morning early, certaine Fowles come and light amongst them, and returne at Night to lodging, which Iland or Ilands are not yet discovered, though probably, by other Reasons they give, there is land, &c.*

— R.W.

Return at night to islands.
Fowl weaving into winds,

                   the wind woven into the quill itself.
A bird
navigating the water's edge, searching the familiar
a vineyard of grapes,

           can remind you of a thing you knew on the body.
A thing perhaps you tasted once

         and through its naming became owner.
This is the benefit of exploration.

| | |
|---|---|
| *Wattàp* | A root of Tree |
| *Wómpimineash.* | Chesnutts. |
| *Wuttáhimneash.* | Strawberries. |
| *Peshaùiuash.* | Violet leaves. |
| *Wenómeneash.* | Grapes. |

Correlation of recognized sense, mapping the body in response to memory and stimuli. The texture of your open eye across my tongue like a new grape with its skin peeled back.

Asqutasquash, *their Vine aples, which the* English *from them call* Squashes *about the bignesse of Apples of severall colours, a sweetness* . . .

— R.W.

It can remind you of a thing you knew on the body,

what you called it in your search for the familiar.
                        Did it relate to a stone, an apple, or element?
The basic paradox of language,
that its inconsistencies should make it most useful.

*"I cannot heare of any disease of the stone amongst them."*

When there is nothing more disparate
than stone from disease,
the apple from Adam, sin from knowledge.

Walk the islands above a waterfall
                        pressing your heels into the silt.

Call this imprint: *Qunnamaúgsuck*—the first that come in the Spring
into the fresh Rivers.

This might mean Lamprey
and there is a consequence.

I have learned to say each word with caution,
                                  your body or any body,
I will not call mine.

    *Wuhóck.*                          The body.
    *Nohòck: cohòck.*            My body: your body.

The first to come
found baskets of corn
                     and brought them away without payment.
To know the feel and taste of a thing
                     as if knowing implies its ownership.

When if both employ the same word,     *mine,*
                   familiarity with language blinds the user to
contradiction,
                   action leads to reaction and consequence.

The next were met and assailed with arrows.

The arrow might remind you of birds
                    and no one can say you are wrong.
The feathered fletching
and obsidian beak.

The history of the word is inseparable from the word
though susceptible to change.

As Augustine:

*"Words are not adopted by men because they have intrinsic meaning, rather
they have a meaning because men have agreed upon them."*

The arrowroot plant
*discovered* in the *New* World
                    was called by the Arawak people: aru-aru
meaning "meal of meals."

The process of the unfamiliar changed to familiar.
Folk etymology refashions the *aru-aru* to *arrowroot,*
                    denies a word of its infinite history.

The shape of a word
cannot save itself from its symbol,
                    that is a pointed leaf
                        or a nectar drawing poison.

Your *demeanor* as *mirror,*
vain thought that conscience
                    denies to speech.

As history changes, we create the history of change.
There is loss,
like a building that rebuilds its facade with the age,
to please the ageless.
Growth is replaced by vanity, if vanity is owning.

The deeds of transfer of their lands by the Indians in Rhode Island are recorded, with the signatures of the sachems appended in the form of their attested marks of a bow, an arrow, tomahawks and other devices, significant of a sign manual.

WINSLOW *Chronicles of the Pilgrims*

To create sign manuals for a life
is a reductive task.
                    They would call it totemic,
a history of emotion and actions, consumed by the sign of a hatchet.
Considering what distinguishes the language of symbol from the
        language of mineral fact,

≈○≈        this could mean island or the man who lives alone.

Deeds become obscure. Possession is transient.

What if no translation exists for the sign?

A bow exists for the English as the shape of the bow itself.
The Narragansett know the bow as *Onúttug*. A halfe Moone in war.

I know you as *pleasure* and the symbol of its origin,
that is not a collective sign.

To affix one's name to a thing
a name which is symbol for a life, which acts as the sign of possession
in conjunction with the thing.


*"The Indians of Martin's vineyard, at my late being amongst them, . . ."*

*Martin* becomes victim to word phenomenon
as *Martha's* Vineyard sees the map,

consider the *aru–aru* . . .

Beneath your white forearm,
the network of vein.
            Unfamiliar, you say *bloodpath*
and I hear *blueprint,*
            because it suits my cause.
To understand
            your arm as bridge, the impossible engineering
written beneath
            your skin.

Island in islands.
Cells course the channels
                    of a  living country,
thick with voyage
                    and the shipwreck of intercourse.
Identical islands
on the span of your chest
                    ringed with riverweed,
red as rock.

*Such sinews even in thy milk, and such things in thy words, . . .*
—Donne

Sinews of the bowstrand,
from the beast itself comes its end.

Its skin retaining the dimensions of the body
and the signature of every wound.

The scar on your inner thigh
is landmark
                    and I might think I've found my way,
call to you.

The way a bird cries out
to travel
        beyond the perimeters of its body.

A note from the sycamore belongs to the field.

What is the open window but an extension of home.

The field as garment,
echoes reclaiming,
          physical shifts below.

     *Mauúnshesh.*          Goe slowly or gently.
     *Taguatchòwash.*       Goe up hill.


Rows of corn
in incessant precision
mould the furrow, at the forehead of every work.

At night to turn and return,
I mould the curve of your back.

Garment gone and naked to the sky,
to the earth spinning gravity,
               your limbs in close around me.

The field and its touch,
familiar surround you,
                  the smell of warm straws
and a light summer mold.

then comfort comes in recognition.

In the billowing of thunderheads
to recognize a hare, a face or an event,
delights the viewer through familiarity.

Of taste or touch,
the fields are flickering with the knowledge of likeness.

The taste of salt
on the inside of your arm
calls to voyage
the shimmering bow as the ship comes in.

The thrill of recognition.

*What cheare* Nétop? *is the generall salutation of all English toward them.* Nétop *is friend.*

Netompaûog.                    Friends.

*They are exceedingly delighted with Salutations in their own Language.*

— R.W.

Every translator has to be two people,
an Indian
        assigned a mark on paper.

A berry-stained moon on a birch palimpsest.

How to paint the name of the moon, which is *Munnánnock*
or the moon itself which is *Nanepaùshat.*

The hemlock on the shoreline
gives up its flat needles
to a vertical line
            topped by a sphere.

Line river on a map
and the loss of its scent,
the gravel sound of suckling
after a surge.

To make maps of a lover's body is
the sad border of a shoulder
                    playing harbour to the head,
not be reconciled
                    by a thin black line.
Or even the broken line
that allows the shifting border,
the dumb index
                    that lacks reflection on the eye.
The compass rose
has lost its magnet
where north is not north
                    but the head on its side.

There is a space between your torso and mine, where travel goes. The charting of my course is instinctual but I give destination no name, as the name for you lacks more than its symbol. You are an island or the name of an island. A name is a bony skeleton, with angles protruding. A ruinous anatomy like the word for swamp, mountain or fish, awaiting the mind to return its mineral matter. Your body doesn't wait for a name, because it has one in the circumference of my arms, where only the skin can speak it.

To steady the body in human intellection,
I relate your parts to home.
Lying in fold, beside this sleeping island,

the nurturing native of your skin,
ribbed rack of meats and warmth from the night

> *In him I have found a House, a Bed,*
> *A Table, Company . . .*

Remembering just how the light stood
on the water surrounding home,

I cannot make love to the same body twice
where the flow of emotion is constant.

Cells charged with melancholy
now vibrate with pleasure.

*Sepûo?*      Is there a River?
*Mishquínash.*    The vaines.

| | |
|---|---|
| *Néepuck.* | The blood. |
| *Wunnícheke.* | The hand. |
| *Wunnáks.* | The bellie. |
| *Mapànnog.* | The breast. |
| *Apòme.* | The thigh. |
| *Sítchipuck.* | The necke. |
| *Wuttòne.* | The mouth. |
| *Wuskeésuckquash.* | The eyes. |
| *Mscáttuck.* | The fore-head. |

The tension surrounding your eyes at the moment life comes to a head.
Nothing planted or harvested but the winnowing of a day's events.
Bark to basket, gathering parts. Island among islands, archipelago.

> *. . . such voyages, such peregrinations to fetch remote and precious*
> *metaphors, such extensions, such spreadings, such curtains of allegories, . . .*
> —Donne

Allegory of conquest, the shipwreck of intercourse.
Alone, the bloody tenant is left to translate history without voice,
a language inherent.